LET'S GO
FISHING
IN A TOURNAMENT

GEORGE TRAVIS

The Rourke Corporation, Inc.
Vero Beach, Florida 32964

PHOTO CREDITS:
© Earl Kogler Corp. Media/International Stock: cover; © Hal Kern/International Stock: page 12; © Greg Voight/International Stock: page 13; © Vincent Graziani/International Stock: page 15; © Wisconsin Department of Tourism: pages 6, 7; ©Tami Heilemann/U.S. Fish and Wildlife Service: page 16; © East Coast Studios: pages 4, 18, 19; © Corel: pages 9, 10

FISH ILLUSTRATIONS: © Duane Raver

PROJECT EDITOR: Duane Raver
Duane Raver received a degree in Zoology with a major in fishery management from Iowa State University. Employed by the North Carolina Wildlife Resources Commission as a fishery biologist in 1950, he transferred to the Education Division in 1960. He wrote and illustrated for the magazine *Wildlife in North Carolina*. Mr. Raver retired as the editor in 1979 and is a freelance writer and illustrator.

EDITORIAL SERVICES: Penworthy Learning Systems

Library of Congress Cataloging-in-Publication Data

Travis, George. 1961-
    Let's go fishing in a tournament / by George Travis.
        p. cm. — (Let's go fishing)
    Includes index
    Summary: Describes different kinds of fishing tournaments and participation in them.
    ISBN 0-86593-467-3
    1. Tournament fishing—Juvenile literature. [1. Tournament fishing.
2. Fishing.] I. Title. II. Series: Travis, George, 1961
Let's go fishing.
SH455.2.T735 1998
799.1'2—dc21   97–51917
                                                      CIP
                                                       AC

Printed in the USA

TABLE OF CONTENTS

FISHING TOURNAMENTS

Fishing is a fun sport. Some people fish in **tournaments** (TOOR nuh munts), or contests for prizes. You can fish alone or with friends as a team.

In most tournaments everyone has to catch the same kind of fish, like a bass or trout. The prize might go to the person who catches the biggest bass or trout.

Anyone who likes to fish can compete in a fishing tournament. For some ocean and lake contests, you must fish from a boat. For others you can fish from the shore. Some fishing tournaments last six to eight hours, or even several days.

These anglers practice for an upcoming tournament.

THE PRIZED CATCH

Each year millions of dollars in prizes are given away to winners of fishing tournaments.

Most people think that money is the best prize. They often spend the money on more fishing gear. Then they have a better chance of winning the next tournament.

This young boy shows off his prize-winning fish, a smallmouth bass.

Prizes usually go to whoever catches the largest fish.

A winner may take home a boat, fishing gear, or a trophy. At some tournaments, the big prize is a fishing trip. Smaller prizes go to people who take second and third place.

BREAKING RECORDS

Fishing tournaments usually have one thing in common: to catch the biggest fish. During tournaments and fishing trips, **anglers** (ANG glerz), or fishermen, try to catch a record size fish.

Catching a record size fish is hard. It almost always means you must break someone else's record. Some records may not be broken for many years.

One of the largest saltwater fish on record is a black marlin. It was caught in Cabo Blanco, Peru, on August 4, 1953. It weighed 1,560 pounds (708 kilograms).

Large billfish like this one are popular tournament fish.

FISHING TEAM

Several big money tournaments give away thousands of dollars for the largest fish caught.

Most contests allow anglers to enter as a team. These contests are known as buddy tournaments. They are important to people who don't own a boat or are trying to catch a fish that weighs hundreds of pounds.

Most teams have a captain, who drives the boat; a first mate, who handles the bait and tackle; and a reelman, who reels in the catch. Working together, these three anglers make a great team.

It often takes teamwork to win a tournament.

CATCH-AND-RELEASE

Because fishing has become so popular, some people worry about overfishing some kinds of fish. Overfishing means that too many of one kind of fish get caught, and too few are left.

Since overfishing has become a problem, many tournaments have a catch-and-release rule. All caught fish must be let go unharmed.

These kids are being shown how to carefully remove a hook.

Fish should be handled gently when returned to the water.

To release a fish safely, remember to:
1. Use a specially designed hook.
2. Keep the fish in the water as much as possible so it can breathe.
3. Never drag the fish in the dirt or handle it too much.
4. Don't touch the gills, fins, or eyes.

PROFESSIONAL EQUIPMENT

Most professional anglers have special equipment for catching prize-winning fish.

Fishing is the best way to find out which gear works best for you. You can also ask longtime anglers for their help in choosing your gear.

First you must ask, what kind of fishing will I do? If fly-fishing in a river, you will need a special type of rod, reel, and line. For surfcasting you will want a longer, stronger rod with a heavier line.

Some anglers use a fish finder. This device helps locate fish underwater.

It takes a lot of practice to become a good angler.

Some of the equipment needed for fly fishing.

FINDING TOURNAMENTS

Many tournaments are held in the United States. The best way to find out about tournaments in your area is to call a local bait and tackle shop or fishing club.

Entering small local tournaments is the easiest way to learn how tournaments work. You will learn how to sign up, the contest rules, and maybe where some of the best local fishing spots are.

For some of the larger tournaments, you may have to travel a long way to enter. This travel can cost a lot of money. These tournaments are better to enter when you become a skilled angler.

This angler caught a fish during a local tournament.

MOUNTING YOUR CATCH

Anglers are always proud of the fish they catch. Some like to take pictures of their catch. Others like to have fish mounted for display.

One method of preserving a fish is **taxidermy** (TAK si DUR mee). A **taxidermist** (TAK si DUR mist) may use the fish's real skin to place over an **artificial** (AHR tuh FISH ul) body. Very little of the real fish is used.

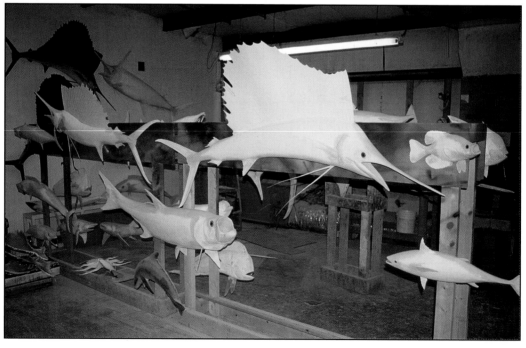

Several game fish are ready to be painted.

This taxidermist is working on a giant tarpon.

Today, some taxidermy mounts use no parts of the real fish at all. The fish is made of fiberglass. Taxidermists use a photograph and the fish's measurements to make the mount.

FISHING SAFELY

When you fish in a tournament, you might be fishing around other anglers. Fishing can be dangerous when you do.

When fishing from shore, make sure that you stay clear of other anglers when they cast their lines. Hooks hurt if they snag you. Also check to make sure all is clear before you cast your line.

When fishing from a boat, make sure you watch for other boaters. In fishing tournaments where you must use a boat, a hundred boats may go out to fish at the same time.

Remember to follow safe boating rules and always wear your life jacket. Fishing safely makes fishing more fun.

fish: bonefish *(Albula vulpes)*
average weight: may reach
10 lbs. (4.5 kilograms)
location: worldwide in tropical
coastal waters

---

fish: king mackerel *(Scomberomorus cavalla)*
average weight: 10 lbs.
(4.5 kilograms), may reach
100 lbs. (45.4 kilograms)
location: western Atlantic from
Massachusetts to Brazil

---

fish: largemouth bass *(Micropterus salmoides)*
average weight: 4 to 5 lbs.
(1.8 to 2.3 kilograms), may
reach 20 lbs. (9.1 kilograms)
location: from Minnesota to
Québec and south to the Gulf

---

fish: redear sunfish *(Lepomis microlophus)*
average weight: 1 lb., 8 oz.
(.7 kilograms), may grow over
4 lbs., 12 oz. (2.2 kilograms)
location: Indiana to the Gulf

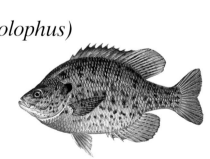

fish: steelhead trout *(Oncorhynchus mykiss)*
average weight: 2 to 8 lbs.
(.9 to 3.6 kilograms)
location: Alaska to
California, northeast
Asia; elsewhere in North
America, Europe, South America, Australia, New
Zealand, Africa, and India

---

fish: white crappie *(Pomoxis annularis)*
average weight: 1 lb. to 1 lb., 8 oz.
(454 to 680 grams), may reach
5 lbs. (2.3 kilograms)
location: eastern North America
from southern Canada to the Gulf

---

fish: wahoo *(Acanthocybium solanderi)*
average weight: 15 to 20 lbs.
(6.8 to 9 kilograms), may
reach 183 lbs. (83 kilograms)
location: most warm temperature and tropical waters

---

fish: white marlin *(Tetrapturus albidus)*
average weight: 75 to 100 lbs.
(34 to 45.4 kilograms), may reach
165 lbs. (74.8 kilograms)
location: Atlantic from Nova
Scotia to Argentina

22

GLOSSARY

anglers (ANG glerz) — fishermen

artificial (AHR tuh FISH ul) — made by human beings rather than nature

taxidermist (TAK si DUR mist) — a person who stuffs and mounts the skins of animals to make them look lifelike, or real

taxidermy (TAK si DUR mee) — the art of preparing, stuffing, and mounting the skins of animals to make them look lifelike, or real

tournament (TOOR nuh munt) — a group of contests, one after the other, in which a number of people try to finish with the best record, such as the biggest fish

INDEX

FURTHER READING:

Find out more about fishing with these helpful books and information sites:
The Dorling Kindersley Encyclopedia of Fishing. The Complete Guide to the Fish, Tackle, & Techniquies of Fresh & Saltwater Angling. Dorling Kindersley, Inc., 1994
Griffen, Steven A., *The Fishing Sourcebook: Your One-Stop Resource for Everything You Need to Feed Your Fishing Habit.* The Globe Pequot Press, 1996
Price, Steven D. *The Ultimate Fishing Guide.* HarperCollins, 1996
Waszczuk, Henry and Labignan, Halto. *Freshwater Fishing. 1000 Tips from the Pros.* Key Porter Books, 1993
Fishernet online at www.thefishernet.com
National Marine Fisheries Service online at www.nmfs.gov
World of Fishing online at www.fishingworld.com